CiA Revision Series

ECDL®/ICDL® Advanced AM6 Presentation

using
Microsoft® PowerPoint

D1428334

Dawn Harvey

Bob Browell

Published by:

> CiA Training Ltd
> Business & Innovation Centre
> Sunderland Enterprise Park
> Sunderland SR5 2TH
> United Kingdom
>
> Tel: +44 (0) 191 549 5002
> Fax: +44 (0) 191 549 9005
>
> info@ciatraining.co.uk
> www.ciatraining.co.uk
>
> **ISBN 1-86005-341-6**
>
> **Release RS04v1**

First published 2005

European Computer Driving Licence, ECDL and Stars Device, ECDL, International Computer Driving Licence, ICDL International Computer Driving Licence and logo, ICDL, and e-Citizen are trade marks of The European Computer Driving Licence Foundation Limited ("ECDL-F") in Ireland and other countries.

CiA Training Ltd is an entity independent of ECDL-F and is not associated with ECDL-F in any manner. This courseware publication may be used to assist candidates to prepare for AM6 Presentation. Neither ECDL-F nor CiA Training Ltd warrants that the use of this courseware publication will ensure passing of AM6 Presentation. Use of the ECDL-F Approved Courseware logo on this courseware publication signifies that it has been independently reviewed and approved by ECDL-F as complying with the following standard:

Technical compliance with the learning objectives of Advanced Syllabus AM6 Version 1.0

The material contained in this courseware publication has not been reviewed for technical accuracy and does not guarantee that candidates will pass AM6 Presentation. Any and all assessment items and/or performance-based exercises contained in this courseware publication relate solely to this publication and do not constitute or imply certification by ECDL-F in respect of AM6 Presentation or any other ECDL-F test.

For details on sitting AM6 Presentation and other ECDL-F tests in your country, please contact your country's National ECDL/ICDL designated Licensee or visit ECDL-F's web site at www.ecdl.com.

Candidates using this courseware publication must be registered with the National Licensee, before undertaking AM6 Presentation Without a valid registration, AM6 Presentation cannot be undertaken and no ECDL/ICDL certificate, nor any other form of recognition, can be given to a candidate. Registration should be undertaken with your country's National ECDL/ICDL designated Licensee at any Approved EDCL/ICDL Test Centre.

Advanced Syllabus AM6 Version 1.0 is the official syllabus of the ECDL/ICDL certification programme at the date of approval of this courseware publication.

Approved Courseware Advanced Syllabus AM 6 Version 1.0

CiA Training's **Revision Exercises** for **Advanced ECDL** contain a collection of revision exercises to provide support for students. They are designed to reinforce the understanding of the skills and techniques which have been developed whilst working through CiA Training's **AM6 -Presentation** book.

The exercises contained within this publication are not ECDL tests. To locate your nearest ECDL test centre please go to the ECDL Foundation website ***at www.ecdl.com***.

Advanced Presentation - The revision exercises cover the following topics, grouped into sections:

- Preparation
- Images and Drawn Objects
- Charts
- Multimedia

- Slide Shows
- Linking
- Macros

A minimum of two revision exercises is included for each section. There are also general exercises, which cover techniques from any section of this guide. Answers are provided at the end of the guide wherever appropriate.

The Revision Exercises are suitable for:

- Any individual wishing to practise advanced features of this application. The user completes the exercises as required. Knowledge of *PowerPoint* is assumed, gained for example from working through the corresponding *AM6 - Presentation* book produced by **CiA**.

- Tutor led groups as reinforcement material. They can be used as and when necessary.

Aims and Objectives

To provide the knowledge and techniques necessary to be able to successfully tackle the features of an advanced word processing application. After completing the exercises the user will have experience in the following areas:

- Creating and adding slides of various kinds to a presentation

- Changing colour schemes and background effects

- Using clip art and drawing tools

- Manipulating images

- Adding animation, sound and video clips

- Creating and editing charts and flowcharts

- Creating and running flowcharts

- Creating and running macros

- Creating links to objects outside the presentation

- Producing custom slide shows

Requirements

These revision exercises were created for *Microsoft PowerPoint*. They assume that the computer is already switched on, that a printer and mouse are attached and that the necessary programs have been fully and correctly installed on your computer. However, in *PowerPoint*, some features are not installed initially and a prompt to insert the *Office CD* may appear when these features are accessed.

Downloading the Data Files

The data associated with these exercises must be downloaded from our website: *www.ciatraining.co.uk/data_files*. Follow the on screen instructions to download the data files.

By default, the data files will be downloaded to **My Documents\CIA DATA FILES\Advanced ECDL Revision Series\AM6 Presentation**. The data required to complete the exercises is in the **Presentation Data** folder and worked solutions for every exercise can be found in the **Presentation Solutions** folder.

If you prefer, the data can be supplied on CD at an additional cost. Contact the Sales team at *info@ciatraining.co.uk*.

Notation Used Throughout This Guide

- All key presses are included within < > e.g. <Enter>

- Menu selections are displayed, e.g. File | Open

- The guide is split into individual exercises. Each exercise consists of a sequential number of steps

Recommendations

- Read the whole of each exercise before starting to work through it. This ensures understanding of the topic and prevents unnecessary mistakes.

- It is assumed that the language selected is English (UK). If this is not the case select Tools | Language, select English (UK) and then the Default button.

- Some fonts used in this guide may not be available on all computers. If this is the case, select an alternative.

- Additional information and support for CiA products can be found at: www.ciasupport.co.uk, e-mail: contact@ciasupport.co.uk

Revision Series
© CiA Training Ltd 2005

Advanced Revision Exercises

Section Exercises

The following revision exercises are divided into sections, each targeted at specific elements of the Advanced ECDL syllabus. The individual sections are an exact match for the sections in the ECDL Advanced Training Guides from CiA Training, making the guides an ideal reference source for anyone working through these exercises.

Preparation

These exercises include topics taken from the following list: knowing how to plan a presentation, considering how to use colour schemes, using background colours and effects, creating, saving and using a template, using a word processed outline for text, inserting slides.

Exercise 1

1. Which of the following may be reasons why different versions of the same presentation would be required?

    a) Audiences with different levels of technical competency

    b) Audiences with different areas of specialist interest

    c) Different length presentations required

    d) All of the above

2. What effect does slide design and appearance have on audience perception of a presentation?

    a) Not at all, content is everything

    b) Minimal, as long as content is clear

    c) Major, can affect how content is viewed

    d) Total, content is irrelevant

3. Give one advantage and one disadvantage of using dramatic images as backgrounds to a presentation?

4. State two considerations when choosing colour combinations to use on slides.

5. Which of the following statements is true?

    a) You can change the colours in a colour scheme

    b) Each Design Template has only one possible colour scheme

    c) All slides in a presentation must have the same colour scheme

    d) Colour schemes depend on slide layout

6. Which of the following would be the most likely reason for supplying a presentation in handout form?

    a) To supply additional information to a presentation

    b) To provide something to read during a presentation

    c) To act as a written reminder of the presentation

    d) To act as evidence that you have attended the presentation

Exercise 2

1. Open the **Cruises** presentation from the data files. This consists of a slide master, a title master and one title slide.

2. Apply the image **Boat** so that it will be the background image to any title slide in the presentation. Why does the colour scheme now need to be changed.

3. Change the pre-set colour scheme for all master slides to one with a dark blue background, pale blue titles and white text.

4. View the slide master and apply a background fill effect. Select the **Nightfall** gradient effect from the preset list. Make sure the effect is applied to the slide master only.

5. Save the presentation as a template called **Cruises.pot**, but make sure it is saved in your data file folder, <u>not</u> in the default **Templates** folder.

6. Now create a presentation based on this template. Insert all the slides from the **Sailing** presentation into the current presentation, making sure they take on the correct formatting.

7. Change the design template for slide 3 <u>only</u> to **Layers**.

8. Save the presentation as **Cruises2** and close it.

Exercise 3

1. Open the **Rocky** presentation from the data files. This consists of a slide master, a title master and one title slide.

2. Apply the image **Rocky** so that it will be the background image to any title slide in the presentation.

3. Edit the current colour scheme so that the title text on all slides will be a very dark blue. Make sure the change is applied to all masters.

4.   Apply a background fill effect that will be applied to all non title slides only. Select the **Parchment** texture effect.

5.   Insert the image **Rockylogo** so that it will appear on every non title slide in the presentation. Enlarge it slightly and move it to the right edge of the title area.

6.   Create four slides in the presentation by importing text from the outline document **Rockytext.doc**, making sure they take on the correct formatting.

7.   Change the background for slide 5 so that the **Rockylogo** graphic is omitted from this slide only.

8.   Save the presentation as **Rocky2** and close it.

Images and Drawn Objects

These exercises include topics taken from the following list: working with drawn objects, changing object backgrounds, rotating, flipping and mirroring images, selecting multiple objects, grouping, ungrouping and arranging objects, cropping and editing images.

Exercise 4

1.   Open the presentation **Camping**. You are to create a revised logo for the Rocky Valley Camping Site.

2. Add a new slide to the end of the presentation with a **Blank** layout. In the centre of the slide, draw an **Isosceles Triangle** from the basic shapes (hold down the <**Shift**> key as the shape is being drawn).

3. Add a colour gradient background to the triangle, from orange at the top to red at the bottom.

4. From the **Flowchart** shapes, draw a **Delay** process. Rotate the shape 90 degrees left and colour it dark green. Resize the shape so that it is small enough to fit inside the triangle.

5. Move the **Delay** shape over the triangle and use Alignment controls to make that the lower edges of the two shapes are aligned, and the **Delay** shape is aligned horizontally in the centre of the triangle.

6. Group the two shapes so that they become one object.

7. Draw a circle just big enough to enclose the triangle and colour it yellow. Move the circle over the triangle make sure that the triangle can be seen on top of the circle. Resize the circle so that it just touches the three corners of the triangle.

8. Group the circle and the triangle object so that the whole picture is one object. Right click the new object and save the image as **Newlogo.gif**.

9. Change the logo on the title master by replacing it with **Newlogo**. Position the image so that it is exactly **21cms** from the left edge and **1cm** from the top edge of the slide. Resize it so that it fits neatly in the title bar

10. Delete the new slide from the end of the presentation.

11. Save the presentation as **Camping2** and close it.

Exercise 5

1. Open the presentation **Camping**. Insert the only slide from the **Eagle** presentation at the end of the **Camping** presentation.

2. Insert the image **Eagle.jpg** into the new slide.

3. Crop the image to include only the eagle's head. As a guide, the final image should be about **5cm** square.

4. Move the image to the right of the text. Use a tool from the picture toolbar to make the majority of the blue sky above the eagle's head transparent.

5. Apply a **Washout** appearance to the image.

6. Use copy and paste to create another copy of the altered image on the slide.

7. Flip the new copy horizontally and move it to the left of the text.

8. Align the two images and the text so that their bottom edges line up and they are evenly distributed horizontally.

9. Align the two images and the text so that they are centered vertically on the slide.

10. Save the presentation as **Camping3** and close it.

Exercise 6

1. Start a new presentation and change the layout of the first slide to **Blank**. You are to create a new graphic to be used in a presentation for the ABC Training Company.

2. Draw a 3cm square shape and colour it dark blue. Apply 3-D Style 11. Use the 3-D Settings to set the 3-D depth to **144pt**.

3. Draw a small text box containing an upper case **A**. Format the character as **Cooper Black** font, size **54pt**, and a font colour of yellow.

4. Move the text box so that the **A** is in the middle of the blue square. Group the square and the text box to form one object.

5. Similarly create a red 3-D box with a **B** on it and a green 3-D box with a **C** on it. Use copy and paste if required.

6. Move the **A** block to the top half of the screen and the **C** block to the lower half, with the **B** block near the centre. Select all three shapes and distribute them so that they are aligned vertically by their right edges and equally spaced.

7. Select all three blocks and group them into a single object. Right click on the object and save it as **abc.gif**.

8. Close the presentation without saving and open the presentation **ABC**.

9. Insert the image **abc** so that it appears down the right edge of all non title slides in the presentation, then run the slide show to see the effect.

10. Save the presentation as **ABC2** and close it.

Charts

These exercises include topics taken from the following list: creating combination charts/2 axes charts, editing charts, creating flowcharts, editing flowcharts, animating charts.

Exercise 7

1. Start a new presentation containing a blank **Title Only** slide. Add a title of **Product Testing**.

2. Create the following flowchart using shapes from the **Flowchart** and **Connectors AutoShapes**. Use text boxes for the **Yes/No** captions.

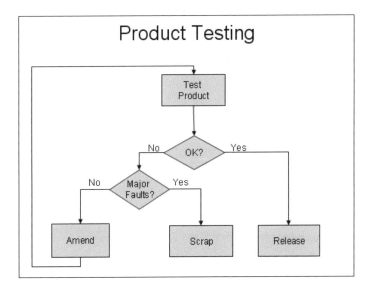

3. Amend the top box of the flow chart to be white text on a dark blue background.

4. Use the **Format Painter** tool to apply this style to all the other flowchart shapes.

5. Change all elbow connectors to **Curved Arrow Connectors**.

6. Save the presentation as **Flowchart** and close it.

Exercise 8

1. Open the presentation **Chart**. The chart shows the year's turnover and profit for a company. Because of the large difference in values, it is difficult to compare them.

2. Change the chart type to a **Lines on 2 Axes** type from the **Custom Types**. The axes should be automatically amended to present the data in a more useful format.

3. Select the **Turnover** data series and change the chart type to 2D clustered column, for that data series only.

4. Without changing any data, change the scale of the **Value Axis** (Turnover) so that it is displayed in **Thousands** with a major unit setting of **5000**.

5. Without changing any data, change the scale of the **Secondary Value Axis** (Profit) so that it is displayed in **Thousands** and starts at **10,000**.

6. Apply an entrance animation effect of **Dissolve In** to the chart.

7. Amend the options for the effects on the slide so that the following sequence is obtained during a slide show:

     First click   Chart background and axes appear

     Second click   Turnover Data Series appears

     Third click   Profit Data Series appears

8. Save the presentation as **Chart2** and close it.

Exercise 9

1. Start a new presentation containing a blank **Title and Chart** slide. This slide will present the average temperature and rainfall for London over the summer months. Add a title of **London Weather**.

2. Add a 2D column chart to the slide and replace the data with the data from the following table:

Summer in London						
	Apr	May	Jun	Jul	Aug	Sep
Rainfall (cms)	3.9	4.5	4.5	5.8	6.0	5.5
Temperature (°C)	8.0	10.0	14.0	17.0	19.0	15.0

3. Change the chart type to a **Line - Column on 2 Axes** type from the **Custom Types**.

4. Add vertical captions of **Rainfall** and **Temperature** to the left and right vertical axes respectively. Move the **Legend** box inside the chart area to the upper right corner.

5. Set the **Rainfall** axis to have a minimum value of **3** and major divisions on the axis representing **0.2cms**.

6. Set the **Temperature** axis to have a minimum value of **5** and major divisions on that axis representing **1.0** degree.

7. Apply a custom animation entrance effect of **Wipe** to the chart.

8. Amend the **Effect Options** so that the following sequence is obtained during a slide show:

    Before clicking   The chart background and axes are already shown.

    First click   Data for the first month (April) is displayed

    Second click   Data for the second month (May) is displayed

    and so on.

9. Save the presentation as **Weather** and close it.

Multimedia

These exercises include topics taken from the following list: inserting sounds and movies, changing animation settings, changing animation sequences.

Exercise 10

1. Open the presentation **Outdoor**.

2. On slide 2 insert an animated clip art image to represent **hiking**. If you cannot locate a suitable image from the *Microsoft* Clip Art galleries, insert **hike.gif** from the supplied data files. This has been extracted from the *Microsoft* media collection.

3. Resize the image so that it is exactly **5cm** high, and maintains the original aspect ratio.

4. Position the image to be **17cm** from the left edge of the slide and **4cm** from the top edge.

5. Insert an animated clip art image to represent **climbing**. If you cannot locate a suitable image from the *Microsoft* Clip Art galleries, insert **climb.gif** from the supplied data files. This has also been extracted from the *Microsoft* media collection. Resize the image to be **5cm** high, **17cm** from the left and **10cm** from the top.

Revision Series
© CiA Training Ltd 2005

6. Apply custom animation to the slide. Add the following entrance effects, all effects to be activated by mouse click:

Title	Faded Swivel.
Bullet Text	Wipe, from left, by 1st level paragraphs
Images	Dissolve In

7. Change the animation sequence to: title, then first bullet text line, then hiking image, then the second bullet text line, then the climbing image.

8. Change the timing so that the title animation starts automatically as the slide opens.

9. Change the timing so that the hiking image appears automatically **1** second after the first bullet text line and then the climbing image appears automatically **1** second after the second bullet text line.

10. Add a sound effect of **chime** to the **hiking** image animation, <u>without</u> inserting a further sound file to the slide.

11. Similarly add a sound effect of **wind** to the **climbing** image animation.

12. Apply settings so that both bullet text lines change to orange when the next animation starts.

13. Show the slide in **Slide Show** view to check the effects.

14. Save the presentation as **Outdoor2**.

15. Close the presentation.

Exercise 11

1. Open the presentation **Sanctuary**.

2. Insert the sound **Scary** from the supplied data files.

3. Make sure the sound will play automatically.

4. In custom animation, set the sound to start playing at the same time as the previous event, and to loop continuously until the end of the slide. Make sure the sound icon is not seen on the slide.

5. Insert the movie **ghost** from the supplied data files. Make sure the movie will run automatically and will loop continuously.

6. In custom animation, set the movie to start playing **1** second after the previous event, and to stop running when the mouse is clicked.

7. Apply an entrance effect of **Fly In** to the lower text box, started by a mouse click.

8. Insert the sound **Laugh** from the supplied data files to play automatically. In custom animation, set the sound to start playing at the same time as the previous event (Shape 2) and not to repeat. Make sure the sound icon is not seen on the slide.

9. Play the slide. The title should animate with sound, then the movie will start moving.

10. Click the mouse to stop the animation and bring in the lower text with new sound.

11. Save the presentation as **Sanctuary2** and close it.

Exercise 12

1. Open the presentation **Captains**.

2. Insert a new slide at the end of the presentation with a layout of **Title, Text, and Content**. Add a title of **New Attraction – Scuba Diving**.

3. Enter two lines of text, **Swim with the exotic creatures of the Coral Reefs**, and **Click to see simulation**.

4. In the area at the right of the slide, insert the movie **fish** from the supplied data files to play automatically.

5. Change the **Effect Options** so that the movie requires a mouse click to start and will loop until the mouse is clicked again. The object is to be hidden when it is not playing.

6. Insert the sound file **Underwater** from the supplied data files so that it plays automatically.

7. Animate the sound to start at the same time as the **fish** animation and to loop until the mouse is next clicked. The sound icon is to be hidden.

8. Show the slide in **Slide Show** view. Click once to start the animation and sound, click again (away from the movie) to stop them both. End the show.

9. Save the presentation as **Captains2** and close it.

Slide Shows

These exercises include topics taken from the following list: creating and editing action buttons, creating and editing custom shows, running a custom ˙show, applying slide transitions, applying timings, setting up a slide show.

Exercise 13

1. Open the presentation **Henderson**.

2. Apply an **Animation Scheme** of **Wipe** to all slides (for *PowerPoint 2000*, apply a **Preset Animation** of **Wipe Right**).

3. Apply a slide transition of **Dissolve** to all slides so that each slide will appear after a delay of **12** seconds, but clicking the mouse button will cause the transition to start immediately.

4. Remove the transition timing from the first slide only so that the first slide will remain on screen permanently until the mouse is clicked.

5. Add a hyperlink on the last text line on slide 5 which will link to the presentation **Products** in the supplied data files folder.

6. Save the presentation as **Henderson2** but leave it open.

7. Change the transition timings to **10** seconds for <u>every</u> slide.

8. Create a **Custom Show** called **Rolling**, which includes slides **1**, **3**, **4**, **5**, **11**, **15**. .

9. Set up a slide show to show the **Rolling** custom show as a continuously looping show to be viewed at a kiosk. The show should run automatically without any intervention and animations are <u>not</u> to be displayed.

10. Amend the **Rolling** custom show to include the original slide **14**, **Summary**. Change the position of the new slide in the custom show so that it is the penultimate slide, i.e. before the **Message** slide.

11. State two command sequences that could be used to run the **Rolling** custom slide show instead of the full presentation.

12. Save the presentation as **Henderson3** and close it.

Exercise 14

1. Open the presentation **Henderson**.

2. On slide **9**, **Benefits Review**, insert a hyperlink on the last text line which links to the document **Handbook** which is included in the supplied data files.

3. On slide **14**, **Summary**, change the hyperlink on the last text line so that it now links to the web site **www.ciasupport.co.uk**. This link can only be tested if an active internet connection is available on your computer.

4. On slide **2**, **Topics**, insert a hyperlink on the first bulleted text line which will link to slide **3**.

5. Similarly insert a hyperlink on the second bulleted text line which will link to slide **7**, a hyperlink on the third bulleted text line which will link to slide **11**, and a hyperlink on the last bulleted text line which will link to slide **14**.

6. Change the link on the second bulleted text line so that it links to slide **8**.

7. Display slide **2** in **Slide Show** view and check the links work correctly. Use the navigation controls to return to slide **2** each time.

8. Edit the colour scheme for the presentation so that hyperlinks and followed hyperlinks are both shown as white text. What feature remains to indicate which text lines on slides are hyperlinks?

9. Create a **Custom** action button in the lower left of slide **7**, **Turnover**. Enter settings so that the button hyperlinks back to slide **2**. Add a caption of **Topics** to the button.

10. Create identical buttons on slides **10**, **Performance Reviews** and **13**, **Required Paperwork**. Use copy and paste if desired.

11. On slide **5**, **Main Products**, add another bullet text line **New Projects**. Add a hyperlink to the line which links to slide **6**, **New projects**. Hide slide **6** from appearing in the slide show sequence.

12. Set up a slide show which will be presented by a speaker, showing all slides, with animations, but which can only be progressed by using the mouse button.

13. Run the slide show from slide **1** and check all links. On slide **5**, **Main Products**, what are the options for moving forward through the show?

14. Save the presentation as **Henderson4** and close it.

Exercise 15

1. Open the presentation **Extreme**.

2. Rehearse timings for the presentation and save them for future use, (no need to be too realistic, a few seconds per slide will be adequate).

3. Create a **Custom Show** called **Excursions** which will include slides **1**, **6**, **7**, **8**, **9**, **10**.

4. Insert the slide from the **Further** presentation at the end of the current presentation.

5. Underneath the first bullet point text, type a suitable web site URL and press <**Enter**>. If you do know a suitable URL, type **www.ciasupport.co.uk**.

6. Typing a valid URL may automatically generate a web site hyperlink to that address. If the text is underlined, edit the hyperlink information and check that the correct site address has been used. What does the application add to the typed URL in the hyperlink dialog box to make the address? If the hyperlink is not added automatically, insert the appropriate web site link manually.

7.   Highlight the word **here** in the second bullet point text and add an e-mail address hyperlink. Make the e-mail address **extreme@ciasupport.co.uk** and add a subject of **Reservations**.

8.   Edit the **Excursions** custom show to include the new slide.

9.   Set up a slide show to be presented by a speaker, showing all slides, no animation and which is advanced by either timings or mouse click.

10. Save the presentation as **Extreme2** and close it.

Linking

These exercises include topics taken from the following list: creating a link to a text file, linking to a chart, linking to a worksheet range, modifying linked data, breaking links and embedding objects, saving a slide as an image.

Exercise 16

1.   Open the presentation **Henderson**.

2.   Insert a new **Title only** slide after slide **10**, **Performance Reviews**, and add a title of **Objectives**.

3.   As the company objectives are in the process of development it is preferable to link to the appropriate document rather than copy it onto the slide. Why?

4.   In the text area of the new slide, insert a link to the file **Objectives.doc** which is included in the supplied data file folder.

5. Increase the size of the inserted object so that it occupies most of the available space and change its background colour to white so that the text can be clearly seen.

6. Save the presentation as **Links1** and close it.

7. Open **Objectives.doc** in *Word* and add another bulleted line: **increase profitability of the company year on year**. Save the file.

8. Open the **Links1** presentation so that any data from linked files is updated.

9. This is now the final version of the objectives. Break the link to **Objectives.doc**, save the presentation as **Links2**, and close it.

10. Open **Links2**. How can you tell there are no longer any active automatic links in the presentation?

11. Close the presentation.

12. Close **Objectives.doc** and *Word*.

Exercise 17

1. Open the presentation **Extreme**.

2. Insert two new **Title only** slides at the end of the presentation and add titles of **Reservations** and **Prices**.

3. Open the workbook **Bookings** in *Excel*. Copy the data range **A1:D17** from **Sheet1** and paste it to the **Reservations** slide as a linked object.

4. Resize the object so that the data is clearly legible.

5. Similarly include the data range **A1:C5** from **Sheet2** as a link on the **Prices** slide and resize it.

6. Save the presentation as **Extreme3** and close it.

7. In *Excel,* change one or two cells of data in **Sheet 1** and **Sheet 2**, then change the background colour of both data areas from yellow to pale green. Save and close the workbook.

8. Open the presentation **Extreme3**, making sure that the data on slides **11** and **12** is current. If you suspect the source data has changed again, what menu commands would start the process to ensure the data on the slides is up to date, without opening and closing the presentation?

9. The price data is now considered fixed. Change the data on slide **12**, **Prices**, so that it is embedded rather than linked.

10. Save slide **12** as an image file **Pricelist.gif**.

11. Save the whole presentation again as **Extreme3** and close it.

Exercise 18

1. Open the presentation **Henderson**.

2. Delete the chart from slide **7**, **Turnover**, and replace it with a link to the chart in the workbook **Turnover.xls**, which is included in the supplied data folder. If **Turnover.xls** and *Excel* were opened in the process, close them now.

3. In the presentation, increase the size of the chart so that it occupies most of the available space.

4. Double click the linked chart to open the source workbook in *Excel*.

5. On the **Data** sheet add a new column for 2005.

2005
35
50
25

6. Check that the chart in the workbook shows the extra data then save the workbook.

7. Check that the chart in the presentation now shows the amended data and resize it again if necessary.

8. Change the properties of the link so that it will no longer update automatically, but will require manual updates. Save the presentation as **Links3** and close it.

9. Open the **Turnover** workbook in *Excel*, change the **Wall** colour of the chart to light blue, then save and close it.

10. Open the **Links3** presentation.

11. By manually updating the link, display the chart on slide **7** to show the latest changes.

12. Save the presentation as **Links3** and close it.

Macros

These exercises include topics taken from the following list: recording a macro, running a macro, assigning a macro to a custom button, removing a custom button.

Exercise 19

Note: For existing macros to work when presentations are opened, macro security
(**Tools | Macro | Security**) must be set to anything but **High**.

1. Open the presentation **Adventure**. Which macros are currently listed in this presentation? Delete them all.

2. View slide **2** in **Normal** view and start recording a new macro with a name of **Picture**. The macro is to be stored with **Adventure.ppt**.

3. Insert the image **Camp.gif** from the supplied data files and use the **Picture** toolbar to set the image colour to **Washout**.

4. Format the picture size to be **13cm** high by **23cm** wide. The **aspect ratio lock** will need to be switched off.

5. Position the picture to be **1.5cm** horizontal and **3.5cm** vertical from the top left corner.

6. Finally use a command to send the image to the back of any stacked display.

7.   Stop recording.

8.   View slide **3** and run the **Picture** macro, then run it again for slide **4**.

9.   Save the presentation as **Macro1** and close it.

Exercise 20

Note: For existing macros to work when presentations are opened, macro security (**Tools | Macro | Security**) must be set to anything but **High**.

1.   Open the presentation **Captains** and save it immediately as **Macro2**.

2.   Start recording a macro called **Handouts** to be stored with the **Macro2** presentation.

3.   The macro is to print handouts for all slides in the presentation. The handouts are to be in greyscale, 3 to the page, on the default printer. If a printer is not available, preview the print instead and leave the print preview window open.

4.   Stop recording and close the print preview window if necessary.

5.   Attach the **Handouts** macro to a new button on the **Standard** toolbar. Include a **Book** icon on the button.

6.   Click the **Handouts** button to check for correct operation. Note if the preview option was taken in step 3, slides may be previewed instead of handouts.

7.   Save the **Macro2** presentation, then remove the **Handouts** button from the toolbar and close the presentation without further saving. Will the **Handouts** button be available the next time **Macro2** is opened?

Exercise 21

Note: For existing macros to work when presentations are opened, macro security (**Tools | Macro | Security**) must be set to anything but **High**.

1. Open the presentation **XYZ** and save it immediately as **Macro3**.

2. Start recording a macro called **Dark** to be stored with the **Macro3** presentation.

3. From the **Slide Design** task pane select **Color Schemes** and apply the scheme **1** (dark brown) to all slides, and then stop recording the macro.

4. Record another macro called **Light** which will apply scheme 8 (white background) to all slides.

5. Add two buttons to the **Formatting** toolbar which will run the **Dark** and **Light** macros. Check the operation of the buttons.

6. Save the **Macro3** presentation then close it.

7. Open the **Captains** presentation and check the operation of the buttons. There is however a basic flaw in these macros. What is it (Hint: Apply a design template of **Eclipse** and check the buttons again)?

8. Remove the **Dark** and **Light** buttons from the toolbar and close the **Captains** presentation <u>without</u> saving.

General Exercises

The following revision exercises can involve processes from any part of the ECDL advanced syllabus.

Exercise 22

1. Why should you consider the target audience for a presentation?

   a) You need to be aware of their subject knowledge.

   b) The tone should be right for the audience.

   c) Both a and b.

   d) Neither a nor b.

2. Which of the following sentences is true?

   a) It doesn't matter what colour background you use.

   b) The text should always be light on a dark background.

   c) The text should always be dark on a light background.

   d) The text should be legible against the background.

3. Open the presentation **Traditions**. Apply the design template **Compass** and save as **Traditions2**.

4. Change the background colour of the image on slide **1** (you will need to click the image twice to edit it, but do not double click) to the same colour as the slide background. Enlarge the image until the dragon's tail overlaps the text, but ensure the text is not obscured by the image.

5. On slide **2**, resize the graphic to twice its original size. Position it at **16.5cm** horizontally and **4.5cm** vertically from the top left corner of the slide.

6. Change the background colour of the sky to dark blue. Ensure the sun is not obscured as a result and that the image is treated as a single object.

7. Apply the sound **china** from the data files to slide **1** (this is a copy of a sound file supplied with *Office*). Ensure the sound plays automatically, but that it stops after the current slide. Drag the icon to the bottom left corner of the slide.

8. Apply animation to the dragon image so that it pinwheels in (**Exciting** effect). Ensure it starts at the same time as the music.

9. On slide **4** apply the same entrance effect of **Rise Up** to the images, triggered by mouse click, so they enter the slide in the following order: **rooster**, **dog**, **boar**, **rat**, **ox**, **tiger**, **rabbit**, **dragon**, **snake**, **horse**, **sheep**, **monkey**.

10. Save slide **4** as an image in **.gif** format to the location where the data is saved, naming it **creatures.gif**.

11. After slide **5**, insert all slides from the **Creatures** presentation. Apply a **bounce** entrance animation effect to the graphic on each of the new slides.

12. Create a custom show called **Overview** from slides **2**, **3**, **18-22**.

13. Attach a custom action button to the bottom right corner of slide **1** to run the custom show, ensuring when the show ends, it returns to the main presentation.

14. Add the text **Main Points** to the button. Resize the button so the text fits neatly. Change the colour of the button to gold and the text to the same colour as the slide background.

15. Apply timings to the show, allowing adequate time for the text to be read and the graphics to be brought in. Do <u>not</u> view the custom show while rehearsing timings.

16. Insert a blank slide at the end of the show and apply a timing of **5** seconds to it.

17. Ensure the show is set up to use timings and then view the slide show (not the custom show at this stage).

18. When the show ends, start it again, this time viewing the custom show. Continue to view the rest of the presentation.

19. Save the presentation with the same name (**Traditions2**) and close it.

Exercise 23

1. Open the presentation **Forest Lodge**.

2. Amend the master slides as follows: on the **Slide Master**, change the master text style to **Tempus Sans ITC 32pt** and the second level text to **Tempus Sans ITC 28pt**. Ensure the **Title Master**, subtitle style is **Tempus Sans ITC 32pt**.

3. Apply a light green colour scheme to all slides.

4. Replace the tree image on all non title slides with the **forest** image from the data files. Ensure the image is positioned at the bottom left corner.

5. On side **3**, change the format of the pyramid diagram to the preset **Gradient** format.

6. The table on slide **7** has been inserted as an image. Print this slide only for reference. Delete the image and change the slide layout to **Title and Table**.

7. Re-enter the data for weekly prices as a table. If the image is obscured by the table, resize the table to prevent this. Centre all text in the table and apply teal (green/blue) coloured shading to row 1 and column 1.

8. On slide **8**, view the data associated with the chart (on the **Data** sheet) and change the year range from **1998-2003** to **2000-2005**. Change the colour of the data series to dark green.

9. Remove the **Price List** slide from the **Public** custom show.

10. On slide **9**, create a link from the text **Click here to read actual testimonials** to the **Testimonials** document from the data files.

11. Apply a **Diamond** entrance effect to the title on slide **1**, so that the **Forest Lodge** text appears with the effect and then dims to pale green after animation. The animation is to work on mouse click.

12. Apply a **Fade Smoothly** transition to all slides in the show.

13. Ensure the slide show is set up to be advanced manually, rather than by using timings.

14. Apply numbers to all slides.

15. View the show without viewing the custom show (via the **Demo** button on slide **1**). Test the link on slide **9**, then close *Word*.

16. View the **Public** custom show.

17. Save the presentation as **Forest Lodge2**.

Exercise 24

1. Open the presentation **Egypt Tours**.

2. Apply a design template of **Cliff** to the slide and title master.

3. Change the colour scheme to sand (light brown) for all masters.

4. On the slide master, change the master title style to **Papyrus 44pt**, master text style to **Papyrus 32pt** and the second level text to **Papyrus 28pt**. Ensure the fonts on the title master have also changed to **Papyrus**.

5. Insert the **profile** graphic to appear as a logo in the top left corner of all slides, including title slides. Resize the graphic to approximately **3.9cm** x **2.6cm**.

6. Use the **Picture** toolbar to set the white background of this image as a transparent colour.

7. On slide **1**, insert a sound file from the **Clip Organiser**, using the **Task Pane** to search only for sound files. Choose any appropriate sound. Ensure it plays automatically, continuously throughout the presentation and that its icon is hidden when not being played.

8. Apply any custom animation effect, animated on mouse click, medium speed, to the text, but not the title, on each slide.

9. Apply a second effect to each graphic (not the logo), so that the text comes in 3 seconds before the graphic.

10. The tour operator has informed you that the **Cairo Museum** is closed for refurbishment. Hide slide **3**.

11. Rehearse timings for the presentation.

12. Create a macro named **Print_Slide** within this presentation only. The macro is to print a single copy of the current slide.

13. Assign the macro to a button at the right of the **Standard** toolbar.

14. Move to slide **7**, **Karnak** and test the button.

15. Set up the show to run using timings. View the show, then save it as **Egypt Tours2**.

16. Remove the button containing the macro from the toolbar.

17. Create a custom show called **Offers** which includes the slides **1**, **2**, **7**, **9**, **11**, **13**. Run the custom show without using the **Set Up Show** dialog box. Which dialog box will be used?

18. Close the presentation.

Exercise 25

1. Start a new blank presentation and apply the design template **Crayons**. The presentation is to promote a further education centre, Chipperstone College.

2. Insert text from the file **Outline**.

3. Change the layout of slide **2** to **Title Slide** and delete slide **1**.

4. Change the size of the master title style to **40pt**, master text style to **28pt** and second level text to **24pt**.

5. Insert the following images from file on to slides **4** to **10**, positioning them at the bottom right of the slide and ensuring they are no larger than the crayons at the left of the slide:

Note: *In XP and 2003, ensure automatic layout is deactivated before inserting the images. Select **Tools | AutoCorrect Options** and the **AutoFormat As You Type** tab. If **Automatic layout for inserted objects** is checked, remove the check and click **OK**. It can be reactivated later if desired.*

Slide 4 - **computer**

Slide 5 - **business**

Slide 6 - **beauty**

Slide 7 - **diy**

Slide 8 - **literature**

Slide 9 - **science**

Slide 10 - **telephone** (flip the phone image horizontally).

6. Insert a new **Title Only** slide immediately after slide **3 Courses on Offer**. Add the title **Pass Rates**.

7. Paste in the chart from the *Excel* workbook **Passes**, ensuring it is linked to the source information.

8. Save the presentation as **College** and close it.

9. Open the **Passes** workbook and change the figures for 2000 to **60** in the **Data** sheet. Save the workbook, but leave it open.

10. Reopen the presentation **College** and update the link. Close **Passes**.

11. Break the link to the workbook.

12. Apply an entrance effect of **Checkerboard** to the chart, medium speed, advanced on mouse click.

13. To each text frame containing bullets, apply an entrance effect of **Fly In From Bottom**, speed fast, so that each line is animated separately. On slide **3**, animate each second level line separately and dim each one to blue after animation.

14. On slide **11**, animate the names to come in 2 seconds after the previous effect.

15. Apply an **Uncover Right** transition, medium speed, to all slides.

General Exercises

16. Run the slide show.

17. Reorder animation for the courses on slide **3** so they appear in alphabetical order.

18. Apply timings to the presentation and set it up to use these timings.

19. Run the show again to check the settings, then save the presentation with the same name and close it.

Exercise 26

1. Start a new, blank presentation, which is to be used as the template for a presentation to promote the local fencing club, The CiA Sabres.

2. Set up the master slides as follows:

   Background - preset **Gradient** fill effect, **Parchment**, shading style **From Title**, variant at the left.

   Slide master - master title style **Tahoma 44pt**, italic, shadowed; master text style **Tahoma 24pt**, picture bullet that co-ordinates with the slide design; second level text **Tahoma 20pt**, picture bullet as above

   Title master - master subtitle style **Tahoma 30pt**

   Slide numbers on all slides.

3. The image **fencer** is to be used on all slides. On the title master it is to be positioned at **0cm** from the top left corner, both horizontally and vertically. On the slide master it is to be positioned **0cm** horizontally and **15.56cm** vertically from the top left corner of the slide.

4. Use the **Picture** toolbar to make the white area of the image transparent on all masters.

5. Save the file as a template named **Fencers** and close it.

6. Start a new presentation based on the **Fencers** template. Add the title **The CiA Sabres** and the subtitle **An introduction to our club**.

7. Create the content by inserting the outline **Sabres**.

8. On slide **4 Equipment**, insert the graphic **mask**. Position it at **15.5cm** horizontally and **8cm** vertically from the top left corner and make the white area transparent.

9. Omit the background image on slide **5 Progression**.

10. Change the layout to **Title Only** and use drawing tools to create a flowchart, illustrating the progression from **Foil** to **Epee** to **Sabre**. Link the flowchart shapes with arrows.

11. Align the shapes and arrows centrally on the slide and then distribute them so they are evenly spaced horizontally.

12. Change the fill of the flowchart shapes to a pale gold colour and group the elements composing the flowchart.

13. On the same slide, insert the graphics **foil** and **epee**. Position **foil** at the left of the flowchart and **epee** at the right. Make the white area of the **foil** graphic transparent.

14. On the title master only, animate the fencer image to come in with a fast **Magnify** effect as soon as the slide appears.

15. Use the slide master to animate all slide titles to come in with a fast **Fly In** effect, from **Bottom-Right** and the remaining text to come in after the title with the same effect. All animations to start on mouse click.

16. On slide **4** animate the graphic to spiral in fast after the text, on mouse click.

17. On slide **5** animate the graphics (**foil** first) to spiral in fast, on mouse click.

18. On slide **9 Club Information** insert the image **kit**. Position it at **16.5cm** horizontally and **6.43cm** vertically from the top left corner.

19. Set the white area as transparent and crop the top part of the graphic so that nothing above the mask is displayed.

20. Create a hyperlink from the e-mail address text on the slide to the stated address (this is a fictitious address).

21. On slide **4**, create a link from the mask image to the following website: **www.leonpaul.com** (a provider of fencing equipment and information). When setting up the link, create a screen tip - **Visit a supplier**.

22. Insert a new **Title Only** slide after slide **8 Sabre** with the title **Demo**. Insert the movie file **Championship**, to play automatically.

Note: Video clip supplied by permission of Leon Paul.

23. Rehearse timings and set up the show to use them. Which menu command and option would you select to suppress animation in a presentation?

24. View the slide show.

Revision Series
© CiA Training Ltd 2005

25. Save the presentation as **Club** and close it.

26. Delete the template **Fencer.pot**.

Exercise 27

1. Open the presentation **Favourites** and add **Favourites** as the title and your name as the subtitle on the first slide.

2. Insert the image **Lake** on to slide **2** and resize it to **10cms** high, maintaining the original proportions.

3. Apply the shadow effect **Shadow Style 6** to the image. Nudge the shadow down and to the right until it can be plainly seen. Colour the shadow green.

4. Use Align and Distribute tools to make sure that the image is positioned exactly in the centre of the slide (horizontally and vertically).

5. Add a right aligned text box underneath the image with the text **Derwentwater from Friars Crag**.

6. Insert the image **Kitten** on to slide **3**. Crop the picture until it just shows the kitten's face, then resize the resulting image to about **8cm** square.

7. Copy the image and paste it three times so that there are four identical images on the slide.

8. Convert one image to **Black and White**, one to **Grayscale**, and one to **Washout**. Arrange the images from left to right in the order **Black and White**, **Washout**, **Grayscale**, with the original image on the far right. Don't worry that the images overlap.

9. Use Align and Distribute tools to distribute the images evenly across the slide both horizontally and vertically, i.e. from top left to bottom right.

10. Change the order of the images so that each one appears in front of the image to its left, as shown below.

11. Apply any entrance animation effect to all four images on the slide.

12. Edit the effects so that the entrance of the top left image is triggered by a mouse click, then each of the other images appears automatically in turn at 2 second intervals.

13. Insert the image **Car** as an embedded object on to slide 4. Reduce the size of the image and move it to the left of the slide.

14. Insert the image **Car** again, but this time insert only a link to the original file. Reduce the size of the image and move it to the right of the slide if necessary to ensure that both images are displayed side by side on the slide.

15. Distribute the two images horizontally across the slide.

16. Save the presentation as **Favourites2** and close it.

17. Open the image **Car.gif** in any photo editing application such as **Paint Shop Pro** from *Jasc Inc*, or the *Microsoft* **Photo Editor**. If there is no photo editing application available to you, rename the image as **Car2.gif** and proceed to step **21**.

18. Use the application to find the current colour depth of the image. What is the next highest colour depth value?

19. Change the colour depth to the next highest value. What command is used?

20. Apply an effect to produce a negative version of the image then save the image as **Car.gif** again. There may be a prompt to change back to 256 colour depth, in which case agree to the change.

Note: To do this exercise again, the original version of **Car.gif** will be required. Either change the amended version back to its original form or reinstall the file from the CD.

General Exercises

21. Close the photo editing application and open the **Favourites2** presentation. On slide 4, one of the images will have changed (or will be missing if the file was renamed in step 17). Which image, linked or embedded, is changed and which remains fixed?

22. Use a format copying tool to apply the style from the **Lake** image on slide **2** to the two images on slide **4**. What is the name of the tool used.

23. Save the presentation as **Favourites2** and close it.

24. If required, to practice image handling techniques, this exercise could be repeated from the beginning but this time using images which represent your own favourite selections. Add more slides such as Favourite Person, Favourite CD if you wish. Save the presentation as **My Favourites**.

Answers

This section contains answers to all specific questions posed in the preceding exercises, together with the name of the file or files containing the worked solution for each exercise.

© CiA Training Ltd 2005

Exercise 1

Step 1   (d) They are all valid reasons

Step 2   (c) Although you could make an argument for b or d.

Step 3   Advantages – Grabs attention, makes an impact, more likely to be remembered.

Disadvantages – Distracts focus from the content, may offend or annoy viewers.

Step 4   Visibility, (no yellow text on white backgrounds)

Consider colour vision impairments

Aesthetics, (no purple text on lime green backgrounds)

Step 5   (a)

Step 6   (c)

Exercise 2

Step 2   Because we now have dark text on a dark background.

A sample solution for this exercise is saved as **Cruises2 Solution.ppt** in the **Presentation Solutions** folder.

Exercise 3

A sample solution for this exercise is saved as **Rocky2 Solution.ppt** in the **Presentation Solutions** folder.

Exercise 4

A sample solution for this exercise is saved as **Camping2 Solution.ppt** in the **Presentation Solutions** folder.

Exercise 5

A sample solution for this exercise is saved as **Camping3 Solution.ppt** in the **Presentation Solutions** folder.

Exercise 6

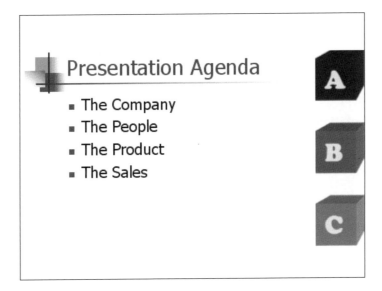

A sample solution for this exercise is saved as **ABC2 Solution.ppt** in the **Presentation Solutions** folder.

Answers

Exercise 7

A sample solution for this exercise is saved as **Flowchart Solution.ppt** in the **Presentation Solutions** folder.

Exercise 8

Step 5

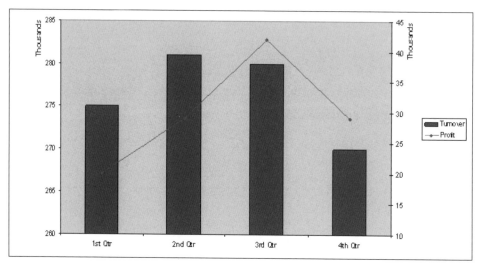

A sample solution for this exercise is saved as **Chart2 Solution.ppt** in the **Presentation Solutions** folder.

Exercise 9

A sample solution for this exercise is saved as **Weather Solution.ppt** in the **Presentation Solutions** folder.

Exercise 10

A sample solution for this exercise is saved as **Outdoor2 Solution.ppt** in the **Presentation Solutions** folder.

Exercise 11

A sample solution for this exercise is saved as **Sanctuary2 Solution.ppt** in the **Presentation Solutions** folder.

Exercise 12

A sample solution for this exercise is saved as **Captains2 Solution.ppt** in the **Presentation Solutions** folder.

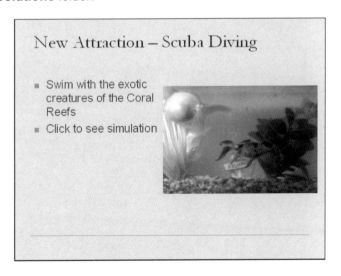

Exercise 13

Step 11 **Slide Show | Custom Shows**, select **Rolling** from the list and click the **Show** button.

Or

Slide Show | Setup Show, select **Custom show** within the Show slides area, and select **Rolling** from the list. Click **OK** then select **View | Slide Show**.

Examples of the output from this exercise are saved as **Henderson2 Solution** and **Henderson3 Solution.ppt** in the **Presentation Solutions** folder.

Exercise 14

Step 8   Text with hyperlinks is underlined.

Step 13   Click on the **New Projects** link to move to slide **6**, or click anywhere else to move to slide **7**. (slide **6** is hidden)

A sample solution for this exercise is saved as **Henderson4 Solution.ppt** in the **Presentation Solutions** folder.

Exercise 15

Step 6   **http://** is added to make the address.

Step 7

 Further Information

- **Further information on outdoor activities can be found at**
  www.ciasupport.co.uk

- **For current reservation data contact us**
  here

A sample solution for this exercise is saved as **Extreme2 Solution.ppt** in the **Presentation Solutions** folder.

Exercise 16

Step 3   So that the presentation will always show the most recent version of the document.

Step 10   Because there is no prompt to update links when the presentation opens.

Examples of the output from this exercise are saved as **Links1 Solution.ppt** and **Links2 Solution.ppt** in the **Presentation Solutions** folder.

Answers

Exercise 17

Step 8   **Edit | Links**.

Step 10

	Weekly Prices	
	July	Other months
Pitches	125	100
Cabin Type A	200	175
Cabin Type B	300	275

Prices

A sample solution for this exercise is saved as **Extreme3 Solution.ppt** in the **Presentation Solutions** folder.

Exercise 18

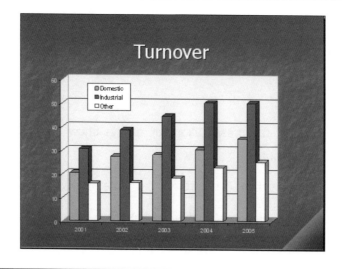

A sample solution for this exercise is saved as **Links3 Solution.ppt** in the **Presentation Solutions** folder.

Exercise 19

Step 1   Macro **Sample** (and **Picture** if this exercise has been previously completed).

A sample solution for this exercise is saved as **Macro1 Solution.ppt** in the **Presentation Solutions** folder.

Exercise 20

Step 7   The button will not be present, it is associated with the application, not the individual presentation.

A sample solution for this exercise is saved as **Macro2 Solution.ppt** in the **Presentation Solutions** folder.

Exercise 21

Step 8   The macros only apply colour scheme 1 and colour scheme 8. In different templates (such as **Eclipse**) these may not be dark and light.

A sample solution for this exercise is saved as **Macro3 Solution.ppt** in the **Presentation Solutions** folder.

Answers

Exercise 22

Step 1   (c) They are both valid reasons.

Step 2   (d).

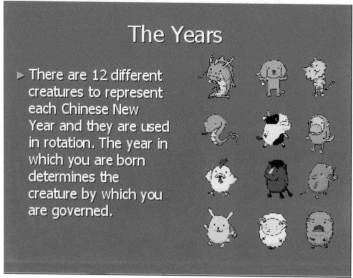

A sample solution for this exercise is saved as **Traditions2 Solution** in the **Presentation Solutions** folder.

Exercise 23

Step 7

A sample solution for this exercise is saved as **Forest Lodge2 Solution** in the **Presentation Solutions** folder.

Exercise 24

Step 17   The custom show can be run from the **Custom Shows** dialog box.

A sample solution for this exercise is saved as **Egypt Tours2 Solution** in the **Presentation Solutions** folder.

Answers

Step 5

IT Courses

- *All popular computer courses are available at the college*
- *Brush up your skills, or start from scratch*
- *Internet and e-mail: learn the essentials*
- *Digital photography and imaging*

A sample solution for this exercise is saved as **College Solution** in the **Presentation Solutions** folder.

Exercise 26

Step 23 Select **Slide Show | Set Up Show** and then check **Show without animation**. Click **OK**.

A sample solution for this exercise is saved as **Club Solution** in the **Presentation Solutions** folder.

Exercise 27

Step 18 **24 bit**, corresponding to 16 million colours.

Step 19 This depends on the application used, for example,

Colors | Increase Color Depth in *Paint Shop Pro*.

File | Properties and select from the **Image Type** drop down list, in *Photo Editor*.

Step 20 The embedded image (on the left) remains unaffected, the linked image (on the right) changes to show the latest version of the source file.

Step 21 **Format Painter**.

A sample solution for this exercise is saved as **Favourites2 Solution** in the **Presentation Solutions** folder.

Note: *In the **Favourites2 Solution** presentation, the second car image is linked to a different file, **Carlink.gif**.*

Other Products from CiA Training

If you have enjoyed using this guide you can obtain other products from our range of over 150 titles. CiA Training Ltd is a leader in developing self-teach training materials and courseware.

Open Learning Guides

Teach yourself by working through them in your own time. Our range includes products for: Windows, Word, Excel, Access, PowerPoint, Project, Publisher, Internet Explorer, FrontPage and many more... We also have a large back catalogue of products; please call for details.

ECDL/ICDL

We produce accredited training materials for the European Computer Driving Licence (ECDL/ICDL) and the Advanced ECDL/ICDL qualifications. The standard level consists of seven modules and the advanced level four modules. Material produced covers a variety of Microsoft Office products from Office 97 to 2003.

e-Citizen

Courseware for this exciting new qualification is available now. Students will become proficient Internet users and participate confidently in all major aspects of the online world with the expert guidance of this handbook. Simulated web sites are also supplied for safe practice before tackling the real thing.

New CLAiT, CLAiT Plus and CLAiT Advanced

Open learning publications are now available for the new OCR CLAiT 2006 qualifications. The publications enable the user to learn the features needed to pass the assessments using a gradual step by step approach.

Trainer's Packs

Specifically written for use with tutor led I.T. courses. The trainer is supplied with a trainer guide (step by step exercises), course notes (for delegates), consolidation exercises (for use as reinforcement) and course documents (course contents, pre-course questionnaires, evaluation forms, certificate template, etc). All supplied on CD with rights to edit and copy the documents.

Online Shop

To purchase or browse the CiA catalogue please visit, *www.ciatraining.co.uk.*

Revision Series
© CiA Training Ltd 2005